Put Beginning Readers on the Right Track with
ALL ABOARD READING™

The All Aboard Reading series is especially designed for beginning readers. Written by noted authors and illustrated in full color, these are books that children really want to read—books to excite their imagination, expand their interests, make them laugh, and support their feelings. With fiction and nonfiction stories that are high interest and curriculum-related, All Aboard Reading books offer something for every young reader. And with four different reading levels, the All Aboard Reading series lets you choose which books are most appropriate for your children and their growing abilities.

Picture Readers

Picture Readers have super-simple texts, with many nouns appearing as rebus pictures. At the end of each book are 24 flash cards—on one side is a rebus picture; on the other side is the written-out word.

Station Stop 1

Station Stop 1 books are best for children who have just begun to read. Simple words and big type make these early reading experiences more comfortable. Picture clues help children to figure out the words on the page. Lots of repetition throughout the text helps children to predict the next word or phrase—an essential step in developing word recognition.

Station Stop 2

Station Stop 2 books are written specifically for children who are reading with help. Short sentences make it easier for early readers to understand what they are reading. Simple plots and simple dialogue help children with reading comprehension.

Station Stop 3

Station Stop 3 books are perfect for children who are reading alone. With longer text and harder words, these books appeal to children who have mastered basic reading skills. More complex stories captivate children who are ready for more challenging books.

In addition to All Aboard Reading books, look for All Aboard Math Readers™ (fiction stories that teach math concepts children are learning in school); All Aboard Science Readers™ (nonfiction books that explore the most fascinating science topics in age-appropriate language); All Aboard Poetry Readers™ (funny, rhyming poems for readers of all levels); and All Aboard Mystery Readers™ (puzzling tales where children piece together evidence with the characters).

All Aboard for happy reading!

To my editor Siobhan Ciminera,
for her insight, enthusiasm, and
wonderful sense of whimsy—G.L.C.

GROSSET & DUNLAP
Published by the Penguin Group
Penguin Group (USA) Inc., 375 Hudson Street, New York, New York 10014, U.S.A.
Penguin Group (Canada), 90 Eglinton Avenue East, Suite 700,
Toronto, Ontario, Canada M4P 2Y3
(a division of Pearson Penguin Canada Inc.)
Penguin Books Ltd, 80 Strand, London WC2R 0RL, England
Penguin Ireland, 25 St Stephen's Green, Dublin 2, Ireland
(a division of Penguin Books Ltd)
Penguin Group (Australia), 250 Camberwell Road, Camberwell, Victoria 3124, Australia
(a division of Pearson Australia Group Pty Ltd)
Penguin Books India Pvt Ltd, 11 Community Centre, Panchsheel Park,
New Delhi - 110 017, India
Penguin Group (NZ), Cnr Airborne and Rosedale Roads, Albany,
Auckland 1310, New Zealand
(a division of Pearson New Zealand Ltd)
Penguin Books (South Africa) (Pty) Ltd, 24 Sturdee Avenue, Rosebank,
Johannesburg 2196, South Africa

Penguin Books Ltd, Registered Offices:
80 Strand, London WC2R 0RL, England

Library of Congress Cataloging-in-Publication Data

Clarke, Ginjer L.
Cheetah cubs / By Ginjer L. Clarke ; illustrated by Lucia Washburn.
p. cm. — (All aboard science reader. Station Stop 2)
ISBN: 978-0-448-44361-4 (pbk)
1. Cheetah cubs—Juvenile literature. I. Washburn, Lucia, ill. II. Title.
QL737.C23C533 2007
599.75'9—dc22
2006018332

10 9 8 7 6 5 4 3 2 1

Cheetah cubs

By Ginjer L. Clarke
Illustrated by Lucia Washburn

Grosset & Dunlap

The sun is setting
on the African grassland.
This cheetah mother sits
on top of a termite mound.
She is looking for
a safe place to sleep.

Her new babies are hiding

in the tall, golden grass.

Can you find the five spotted cubs?

The cheetah's spots help it
blend into the grass.
The name cheetah comes from
the Indian word "cita" (say: chee-tuh).
It means "spotted one."

Every cheetah has a different
pattern of spots.

Just like the way your fingerprints
are different from everyone else's.

Cheetah cubs look soft and cuddly,

but their coats are actually

thick and scratchy.

Only the fur on their spots is soft.

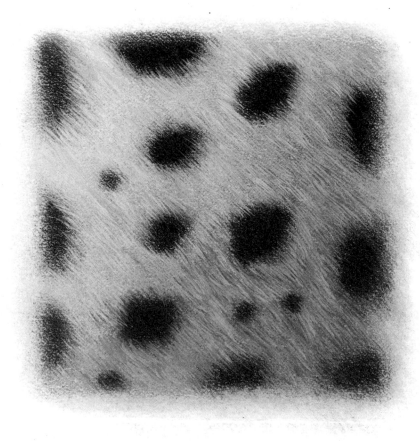

Cheetah cubs also have

longer fur around their necks.

This is called a "mantle."

It helps them blend into the grass.

This makes it harder

for predators to see them.

Uh-oh!

The cheetah mother sees a hyena.

Hyenas, lions, and leopards can hurt

cheetah cubs that are left alone.

Cheetahs cannot roar like lions.

So the mother hisses and arches her

back to frighten the hyena away.

Then she calls to her cubs

with a soft chirp to tell them

to keep still and stay together.

The hyena could come back anytime.

So the cheetah mother

has to move her cubs quickly.

She uses her teeth to gently

pick up one cub by its mantle.

Then the mother runs away
with the cub to find a hiding place.
She comes back again and again
until all of the cubs are safe
in a den nearby.

Now the cheetah cubs
are sleeping snugly.
They will stay here until their mother
moves them in the morning.

The cheetah mother moves her cubs
almost every day to keep them safe.
But for now, the cubs take a catnap.

When the cubs wake up,

they greet one another.

They sniff, lick, and rub cheeks.

The cubs clean one another
with their rough tongues.
They purr just like kittens.

It is time for breakfast.

The cheetah cubs cuddle

next to their mother.

They drink her milk hungrily.

The mother will feed her cubs milk

for about three months.

The cheetah mother leads her cubs

out of the den into the sunlight.

The cubs are ready to play.

They spin and leap.

They climb and chase.

They even play leapfrog!

The cubs will use these skills

when they start hunting.

Cheetahs like to play,
but they are usually shy.
They do not attack humans.
A long time ago, some rich
people kept cheetahs as pets.
People also trained cheetahs
to hunt for them.

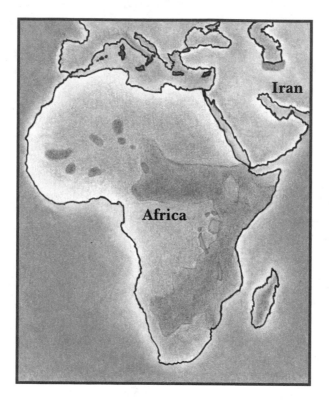

Today, people are dangerous to cheetahs.

They kill cheetahs with guns

for their beautiful fur.

And because people live everywhere

in the world now,

cheetahs have less land

to live and hunt on.

Cheetahs used to be common
in many parts of the world.
Almost 100 years ago,
there were 100,000 cheetahs.
But now they are rare.
Only about 12,000 cheetahs are left.
They live only in Iran and in
southern and eastern Africa.
Many cheetahs also live in zoos.

The cubs are three months old now.

Their mother stops feeding them milk.

She brings them the animals

that she catches.

She will share her catches until the

cubs learn how to hunt on their own.

Cheetahs eat impalas, gazelles,
antelopes, rodents, and rabbits.
Cheetah cubs need to eat
fresh food every day.
So their mother works very hard
when she goes out to hunt.

Cheetahs are good hunters
because they are very fast.
They are the fastest land animals.
They can run up to 70 miles per hour!
That is more than twice as fast as
the best human runners.
Even a racehorse can only run
about 45 miles per hour.

Cheetahs can reach their top
speed in about three seconds!
But they get tired quickly
and can only run this fast
for up to one minute.

Cheetahs are built for speed.
Their backbone stretches
like a spring.
They have long, strong legs.
Their claws help them dig
into the dirt like
spikes on soccer shoes.

Their heart and lungs are larger than
those of other big cats to help them
breathe while they run fast.
A long tail helps them balance.

Even the dark stripes
on their faces are helpful.
The stripes keep sunlight
out of the cheetah's eyes.

Other big cats, like lions,

hunt in packs.

But cheetahs work alone

to catch their prey.

The mother cheetah stalks
a herd of antelope.
When they see her,
they scatter and run.

The mother cheetah chases an antelope

until she catches up to it.

She swats the antelope

and knocks it down.

She grabs it by the throat

with her strong jaws

to stop it from breathing.

After the chase, the mother cheetah

has to rest for up to 30 minutes.

She pants like a dog to help her

cool off from running.

Then she eats fast before

another animal steals her food.

She takes some of her catch

back to her hungry cubs.

The cheetah cubs are eight

months old now.

It is time for them to learn to hunt.

Their mother brings them

a live rabbit to practice on.

At first, they think they are

just playing a game.

They squeal and run in circles.

They do not try too hard

to catch the rabbit.

After much practice,

the cheetah cubs are ready

to hunt on their own.

They spot a pack of gazelles

and run toward them.

One of the cubs comes close

to making a catch.

But the gazelle is too fast.

This cub is tired from the chase.

He stops to rest in the shade.

He will wait a few hours

before trying to hunt again.

Later, the cub sees a young gazelle
without its mother.

This time, the cheetah cub is faster
and catches the gazelle.

Now the cubs are
one-and-a-half years old.
It is time for their mother
to leave them.

The cubs will stay with one another
for a few more months.
They keep hunting as a group.
They still play sometimes, too.

A few more months go by.

The cubs are two years old now.

They are grown-up cheetahs.

The male cheetahs will live in a group

together for their whole lives.

But the female cheetahs
leave their brothers.

Each female cheetah goes off alone.

It is time for them to find mates
and start new families.

Soon one of the female cheetahs

has cubs of her own.

The cubs tumble and leap.

They wrestle and roll.

Time for more cheetah cub fun!